Come Learn About
Dolphins

by Stephanie Wilder

Scott Foresman
is an imprint of

PEARSON

Glenview, Illinois • Boston, Massachusetts • Chandler, Arizona
Upper Saddle River, New Jersey

ISBN 13: 978-0-328-51660-5
ISBN 10:   0-328-51660-0

4 5 6 7 8 9 10 V0FL 14 13 12 11

Do you ever wonder about **dolphins?** Would you like to swim through the ocean and take a few **glimpses** of the secret world of dolphins? Today you can!

Scientists have been studying and working with dolphins for years. We now know more than ever about how they live and play. Together we will make an expedition to the deep sea and find out more about the secret life of dolphins.

Dolphins like to swim in warm water, but they can adapt to live almost anywhere. Bottle-nosed dolphins, the most common kind of dolphin, live in the Atlantic, Pacific, and Indian Oceans, as well as the Mediterranean Sea. They live all over the Atlantic Ocean, from Cape Cod to the Gulf of Mexico and the African coast. In the Pacific they can live as far north as Monterey, California.

Some dolphins live close to shore, and others live far out at sea where the water is colder. Dolphins have a layer of blubber that helps them keep warm in chilly water. Their heart rate and blood flow adjust to their needs. The heart rate speeds up or slows down depending on how much body heat is needed.

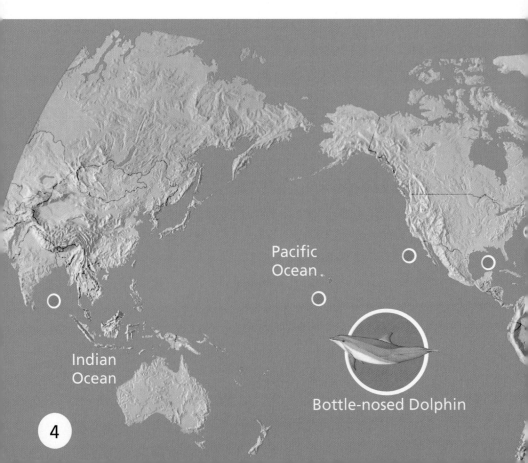

Pacific Ocean.

Indian Ocean

Bottle-nosed Dolphin

Dolphins can grow to be twelve feet long and weigh as much as one thousand pounds. They may look like fish, but they are mammals. They have to come up to the **surface** of the water to breathe. Dolphins breathe through blowholes. This is the little hole on the top of the head. This way a dolphin can breathe air while keeping its body hidden underwater.

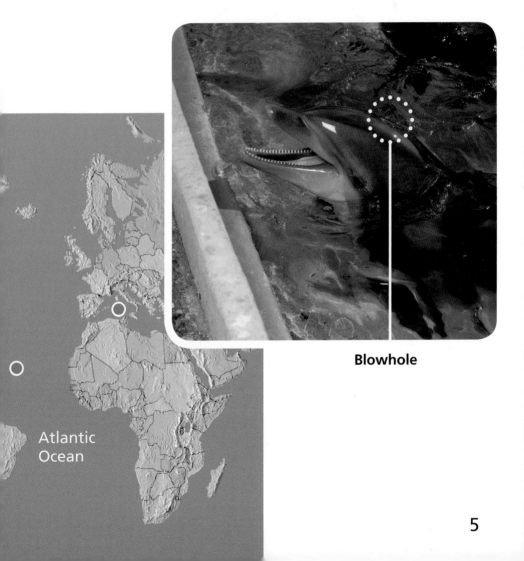

Blowhole

Atlantic
Ocean

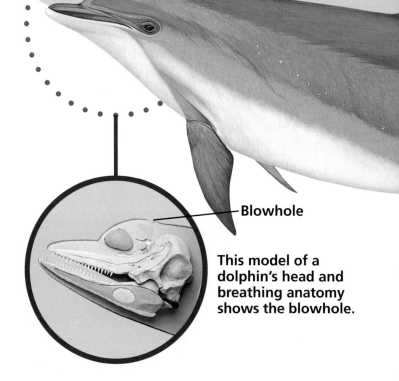

Blowhole

This model of a dolphin's head and breathing anatomy shows the blowhole.

Dolphins dive and surface to breathe.

Dolphins are able to hold their breath for up to ten minutes! This allows them to dive down deep to find food and explore the ocean.

So how can dolphins hold their breath so long? A dolphin is able to lower its heart rate when it dives. A lower heart rate allows a dolphin to save oxygen. Also, a dolphin is able to pull blood away from its flippers and bring it into its heart. The more blood around the heart and lungs, the longer a dolphin can stay underwater.

As dolphins dive, the water around them puts a lot of pressure on their bodies. But dolphins are used to it. Normally, they can dive as deep as 150 feet, but they have been known to dive much deeper under experimental conditions.

Dolphins use their special breathing skills to hunt for food. In the wild, dolphins eat all kinds of fish, squid, and shrimp. Raw fish is a dolphin's best dinner.

Dolphins do not chew their food the way some mammals do. They have teeth, but they only use them to break up big pieces of food. They swallow little fish in one big gulp. Most of the time dolphins swallow the fish headfirst.

This dolphin may feed on the school of fish.

Dolphins work together to find food. In deep water a big group of dolphins might get together to surround a whole school of fish. Next, they take turns swimming through the school of fish and feeding on them. In shallow water the dolphins might chase the school of fish to the shoreline, where it is harder for the fish to get away.

Dolphins also hunt for big fish that swim alone. Dolphins use their **flexible** tail flukes to hit the fish and slow them down. Sometimes dolphins follow fishing boats, eating the fish that free themselves from the nets.

Dolphins are able to find their food, and even find fishing boats, with their senses. Dolphins can see, hear, taste, and feel.

Dolphins have very good eyesight. They can see both in and out of the water. A special lens in their eyes helps them adjust to the changes in light.

Dolphins do not have olfactory lobes, which are important for an animal's sense of smell. Most scientists think that dolphins do not have a strong sense of smell.

Dolphins may not be able to smell their food, but they can hear it coming. Dolphins actually use their jawbones to detect sound waves in water. They do have small ear openings, but their jaws are more important for detecting sound.

Dolphins use echolocation to find fish in the deep, dark waters of the ocean. Echolocation is a way for dolphins to find objects by sending out **pulses** of sound that echo off them. Dolphins make a clicking sound. The sound waves from the clicks bounce off nearby fish. The dolphins wait to feel the echo come back. Then they are able to tell what is in front of them.

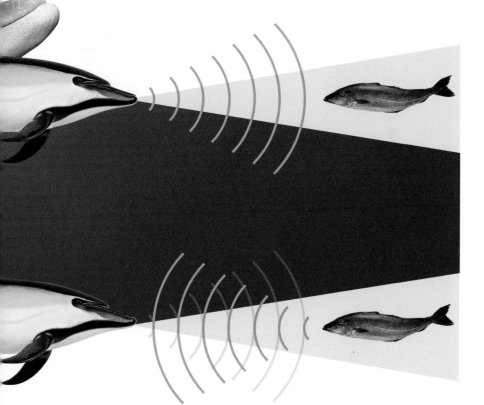

Pulses of sound from the dolphin echo, or bounce, off of the fish so the dolphin can find and catch it. This is called echolocation.

Dolphins form very close family groups called pods. Dolphin pods stay together for a long time. The size of a dolphin pod changes depending on where the dolphins live. Usually these groups include a few female dolphins and their young. The male dolphins travel together. Some adult males briefly join different female pods.

Sometimes a pod is made up of dolphins of the same family. Some dolphins of different families may come together out of a need for protection.

Sometimes several pods will come together to form a herd. A herd can have several hundred dolphins! The herds will stay together for a few hours to hunt or for protection.

Dolphins swim together in a pod.

Like all mammals, a baby dolphin, or calf, grows inside its mother. When a baby dolphin is born, it can be five feet long and weigh up to forty-four pounds!

When the calf is born, its fin and tail flukes are soft. After a few days the fin and flukes finish developing and become harder. The baby drinks milk from its mother for more than a year, but it also starts to eat fish after just a few months.

A calf has to wait a few days before it can make noise. But before long it can make the same noises as grown-up dolphins. The calf stays with its mother, learning to swim and hunt, until it is fully grown. All dolphin calves need their mothers to take care of them and teach them new things.

Mother dolphins communicate with their babies and the other members of the pod through whistles. Mothers whistle to their calves until the calves are able to distinguish them from other dolphins in the pod. Scientists think that these sounds come from the nose of the dolphin. Sometimes the noises dolphins make sound like moans and creaking doors. They can make them in and out of water.

Scientists do not know if other animals can hear dolphin noises. But they do know that dolphins sometimes play with other toothed whales like themselves.

Bottle-nosed dolphins will travel with other dolphins and even with pilot whales. They sometimes follow bigger whales to ride in the waves they make. Dolphins have been seen with gray whales, humpback whales, and right whales.

Dolphins don't make friends with sharks, but they do not hide from them either. Sometimes bottle-nosed dolphins will even attack and kill smaller sharks, such as tiger sharks. Dolphins are good hunters. If they work together they can attack these sharks, but most of the time they just avoid them. They play with other dolphins, catch fish to eat, and enjoy the water.

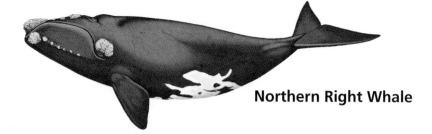

Northern Right Whale

Dolphins are friendly animals when it comes to most other sea life. They are also friendly with people.

Sometimes wild dolphins can be seen riding in the trail of boats. Sometimes they even let people touch and swim with them. But be careful; some dolphins are not as nice as others. They are still wild animals, and their behavior can be aggressive. When scientists study dolphins in the wild, they always take care not to put themselves or the dolphins in danger.

A scuba diver swims with the dolphins.

It is usually safe for humans to have contact with dolphins that live in an **aquarium.** You may have seen pictures of marine biologists swimming in tanks with dolphins. These animals are playful and very gentle.

Dolphins that live in aquariums can learn to do all sorts of tricks to entertain crowds of people. They can also help scientists learn more about their daily activities.

Scientists have learned a lot about how dolphins act with their babies and other dolphins by watching what they do in aquariums. They can see the dolphins when they eat, sleep, and play. They can see when dolphins are healthy and when they are sick.

This dolphin is being trained as part of an aquarium show.

By listening to the sounds dolphins make and by watching them jump as high as sixteen feet in the air, scientists have been able to learn more about the ways they communicate and play with each other. Their sounds and actions send signals to other dolphins about food and fun.

Scientists used to think that they could learn to speak dolphin language and that dolphins could learn to recognize the sounds that humans make. This has not worked. Dolphins can learn to respond to humans but not to their words. Scientists and trainers have been able to teach dolphins to do all sorts of things by rewarding them with fish when they perform.

Dolphins perform tricks for humans all over the world. Trainers teach them to jump high out of the water and to carry people on their backs. These tricks are all versions of the tricks dolphins play in the wild with each other.

Most of the dolphins we see in aquariums were born there. But many of their actions are still like those of dolphins found in the wild. They still play and enjoy social activities with other dolphins.

There are many things that scientists would not be able to study and learn if they were not able to observe dolphins in aquariums. New studies are happening all the time. The information we have about dolphins is growing every day. Recently, scientists learned that dolphins can see themselves in mirrors. This is a trait that very few animals have.

Dolphins have adapted to their lives in the ocean. Dolphins live underwater, but in many ways they are like mammals that live on land. They breathe the same air and form the same strong family bonds as many other mammals.

Dolphins live in an **enchanted** world. They spend their days gliding through the ocean, exploring things most people will never know. By understanding the secret life of dolphins, we can learn more about the secrets of the ocean.

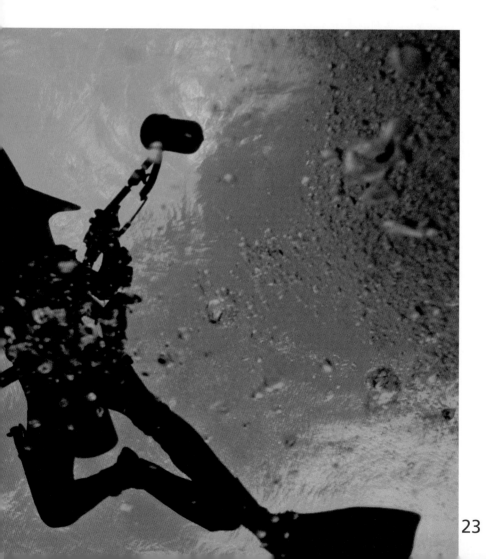

Glossary

aquarium *n.* building used for showing collections of live fish, water animals, and water plants.

dolphins *n.* sea mammals related to the whale, but smaller.

enchanted *adj.* delightful; charming.

flexible *adj.* easily bent; not stiff.

glimpses *n.* short, quick viewings or looks.

pulses *n.* a regular, measured beat.

surface *n.* the top layer.